In The Eyes
Of A Veteran's Daughter

Jordan Kay Leininger

To order additional copies of this book, contact:

Jordan Kay Leininger
5907 Mile High LN
Midland, Texas 79706

Published by FWB Publications
Columbus, Ohio

FWB

Introduction

Do soldiers really know what their life as a veteran will be? And if they did would they ever become a soldier? The difference between a soldier and a veteran is not a big difference. The soldier is active duty and a veteran is not active any longer. Both served our country well but the veteran is the one we forget about.

My Dad
Joseph Lewis Strong

Jordan Kay Leininger

Abstract

Quality of life of a veteran is sometimes not as it was as a soldier. Has America forgotten our veterans once were soldiers? Of course they have, our veterans are forgotten. Approximately 100,000 are homeless. It should sicken Americans to know our past soldiers that served our Country now are homeless veterans. As a young girl I experienced my dad as a productive soldier full of life and ambition to accomplish anything. Unfortunately those years didn't last long enough. Every little girl dreams of her dad to always be there mentally and physically for her through the years. Never did I dream my dad would be dependent on my mom and me and my sister. It all started in Fort Bragg, North Carolina, and continues in a small town in Oklahoma.

Table of Contents

Chapter 1

Remembering the Soldier

It all starts on a fall day in November, 1978, Fayetteville, North Carolina, Ft Bragg, Joseph Lewis Strong joined The 82.

My dad served three years before he and my mom married in December, 1980. Little did my mom know what the future held. Two years later I was born in the summer of 1982 to a soldier and my mom. Cape Valley Fear Hospital Fayetteville, NC. I believe my dad had hopes for a boy but I stole his heart.

My Dad would continue to dedicate his time to the army. It was his way of life, helping friends and giving 100% to the army. And he made time for me and my mom. We didn't mind that he dedicated his time to the army, it was his job and that made him happy. And a better husband and dad.

Twelve months after my birth my sister was born. A blessing but we are very close in age. My parents were excited to be blessed with two girls. Not their plan but Gods. My dad continued being a dedicated soldier.

He would have BBQs and we would get to know his military buddies. He would also, on occasion, take me and my sister to the military base. My mom had a job to help support our family. That's a major problem with being in the military and fighting for your country and protecting Americans, you don't make enough money to support a family. We pay other people for football and other sports that entertain Americans. But our military that protects Americans always suffers.

I hear Bruce Springsteen playing on the radio "Born in the USA" while in the car with my dad. I felt proud to be an American and proud my dad was serving our country. My sister and I had a great childhood growing up. Our parents always took us on vacations. We would go to Myrtle Beach a lot. Those were some of the best days of my life. My dad spoiled my sister and me.

My dad also taught us never to ask anyone for anything. And always to respect others. Also, we had to refer to people as ma'am or sir. But we had it down because my dad was a good example of that. At the time my sister and I thought he was crazy, but now I realize he wasn't crazy at all.

Chapter 2

Learning to Deal

As a little girl growing up I watched my dad as a soldier help clean and cook and take care of me and my sister. I always thought my dad would be there. Little did I know in 1991 my dad would become a veteran due to Post Traumatic Stress Disorder (PTSD). I had no idea what was about to happen. We would move from North Carolina to Broken Arrow, Oklahoma. Definitely a change in atmosphere.

As a little girl I had no idea my dad would be there physically but not mentally. How do you explain that to kids? After the move my dad would get a job but struggle with depression. He would blow it off until he lost his job. We moved once again from Broken Arrow, Oklahoma, to the small town of Muldrow, Oklahoma. We had family there, a big support system. My dad took a postal exam, scored perfect on the exam, but didn't get the job. Talk about a big let-down to him. He went from working every day to not working. Then he struggled with reality, he went from being outgoing to a deep depression.

My dad struggled with the whole life issues. As I am growing up, I'm seeing my dad who used to be strong and independent become dependent on everyday skills. We would have to help him with simple tasks. Most days he would sleep his life away. He would see a physiatrist once a month, all they did was medicate which caused him to be happy but sleep all day.

Chapter 3

Daddy's Girl for Life

As a daddy's girl I'll always remember the soldier he was. That he was a normal dad, fun, outgoing, funny, and full of life. But that soldier turned into a veteran. My dad would become dependent on my mom and sister. He knew he became dependent and to him his life was worthless.

He would become 100% disabled as well as diabetic. His depression had gotten so bad he would end up in the mental institution because he would be suicidal. His pills would make him sleep all day. My mom and sister and I would visit him in the mental ward many times. He would get better and regulated on meds, and get to go home. But it would be short lived, he would be back and forth for so many years.

It stressed my mom out bad. Most people would have been gone. But my mom held to her marriage vows in sickness and health and my dad had a sickness.

It's hard seeing your parents or parent who raised you act like a kid themselves. One day my dad was introduced to drugs, we had no idea what was about to happen. He all of a sudden became full of energy and the dad we used to know. But that came to an end quick. He would go missing for days, even weeks, and we still had no idea. We would worry sick about if he was dead or hurt.

It took an emotional effect on me and my mom. Finally we got a call that he was in jail and on drugs, he had been living basically on the streets. Back to rehab he would go and regulated on new meds and he would come back home. But he would refuse to take his meds. So he would not take them and get back on the streets and use drugs. By this time my sister and I are teens. He became verbally abusive to my mom and me and my sister. It was the drugs talking. I laid awake at night wondering if he would come home and kill my mom or all of us or himself. You hear all the time where people in the military kill themselves or their family.

Chapter 4

The Veteran on the Streets

People took advantage of my dad who is a veteran. As the years went by I would marry and have a baby. My dad would still be in and out of rehab and on the streets and on drugs. Also in trouble with the law. He would promise he would change and he kept it for a couple of years.

But he would relapse back on drugs, his depression would worsen and diabetes would diminish his health. It's hard seeing your dad on the streets doing crazy things and not caring about his family or his own life. Finally his last round of rehab straightened him up and he got regulated on meds. He needed 24-hour care but he lacked one day of war time to be placed in a soldier's home. Basically the VA's way of saying "you deal with him."

My mom had a good job to give it up and care for my dad who didn't get much money on disability. She had credit card debt to pay off that my dad did while on the streets, a mortgage and a car payment. But he had to have someone there to make him take his meds and make sure he didn't go with people he wasn't supposed to. Or he would end up on drugs again and maybe dead on the streets.

Chapter 5

Never Giving up Hope

I would be the one to take care of him and get him to his appointments. By this time I had two kids in school and one on the way and finishing up college online. I finally came to the realization that my dad would never be the same. I'd be responsible for him and take care of him. Have I thought about if he never joined the army?

Every day I think of how things would have been different if he never joined. I know he wouldn't be mentally messed up or physically messed up if he never joined. And never dependent on my mom or my sister and I. Do all veterans suffer the consequences of being a soldier and going to war? Yes they do, especially if they never received the proper treatment.

Even if my dad received proper treatment from the VA he probably would have overcome his depression and been a halfway normal person. But that wasn't the case at all. I'd soon see it for myself. I would take my dad to his appointments at the VA. I would see all kinds of veterans. Talk about sad, we Americans have the slightest idea how our veterans are being treated.

Chapter 6

The Lack of Care

Let's just say when I took my dad to appointments the doctors would treat him like crap. Like it was his fault he was a veteran. I had to sit in on his appointments so I could tell my mom how he was doing. Not only were the doctors disrespectful, the clinic and VA hospital looked like trash. Like something you would see in a movie.

Veterans standing everywhere waiting to be seen, almost like an assembly line. It was horrifying to know the people that fought for our freedom were being treated worse than our prisoners. My dad was disrespected several times but he still gave respect. My dad never liked taking the pills his physiatrist prescribed.

Chapter 7

Freedom isn't Free

The reality is he had to take the pills to socialize with others. They made him sleep. So I am sitting in on one of his appointments with his physiatrist. The doctor asked how everything has been, and dad would reply he doesn't want to take his medicine. The doctor, to my surprise, stated "Well you don't have to. "

I am no doctor but I'm smart enough to know when my dad is not responsible for his own actions he needs his meds. And that he can't make decisions because he is incompetent. That's why he has 24-hour care. Regardless what that doctor told him, me and my mom made sure he took that pill, and followed it with B12 so he wouldn't be so tired.

Basically our veterans get the worst care of anyone else, I quickly learned. They would miss-diagnosis so my mom got him a regular doctor through her insurance. He would find things the VA missed or really never tested for to begin with. The VA would treat him after the regular physician found the problems. Not the best treatment, I would have to say.

Me and my dad grew closer again I would take him to his appointments and he would go to my prenatal appointments. We would hang out at the house and go across the road to my aunts to have lunch with her. I would do my college online while he was sleeping. We would go grocery shopping together. He loved being out of the house and I don't blame him. Same routine every day gets old.

Every evening when I'd go home my mom would be home and she was responsible for his night medicine. He also had high cholesterol, high blood pressure, and he was diabetic and took insulin. We had to check his sugar because of him being incompetent. If we forgot his sugar would get in the four hundreds.

Chapter 8

Never Give up on a Veteran

My mom felt like she was raising a kid all over again. We had to tell him to take his medicine and to take showers. We had to cook the right foods so his diabetes would stay under control. I would get my kids ready for school, go to my parents' house, run in, give my dad his medicine, and he would go with me to take the kids to school. We would eat breakfast and go look around at different stores.

He was like a kid, he loved to look around at different things. He never talked much like he used to. I found out five months into my pregnancy that I had gestational diabetes. So I basically ate the same diet as my dad and had to check my blood sugar as well as his. The only difference being that I controlled mine with my diet, and he had insulin. College got harder and at times my dad got irritated because he had become dependent.

Every day for him was the same. It was very different from when he was a soldier, outgoing and traveled. He traveled with my mom but he never looked forward to it. He used to love the car rides. It's kind of sad to see your dad like that. It's even sadder to see anyone that served our country on the streets. They put their lives at risk, would have died for all of us and they didn't have to. But we won't help them?

Chapter 9

The Forgotten Soldiers

Did we forget they served our country and that's why we are free? My dad would see many physicians over the years and nothing really helped. It was like the VA would just medicate him. And he seemed like he was zoned out all the time. He never talked, just stared.

We would ask his doctor if there was anything that would not make him so zoned out. It was almost like he had Alzheimer's disease, and that at times was hard to see. The doctor basically said to keep him medicated or he would relapse. To me that was a slap in the face. Of course the doctor would want to medicate him, it's easier than trying new treatments that might help. But this is occurring at the VA where so many veterans look medicated. I was wondering if this is the treatment you get for serving your country, it's not worth it.

Chapter 10

Heartache of Freedom

How many family members actually take care of the veterans with a mental disorder? Not very many, that's why a lot of them are homeless. Because veterans refuse treatment a lot of times, they suffer from alcoholism and drugs trying to forget what they have seen. And the family suffers until they have had enough.

There is a side of me that wonders if we let him go and not cared or just felt we couldn't handle him, where would he be? Don't get me wrong, there were plenty of times we all wanted to throw in the towel and be done with it all. It was hard, he would have honestly been on the streets or dead if we gave up.

And I don't think we could have lived with ourselves knowing he had a mental disorder and we let him go. It's not like he had always been like this, he wasn't. I wanted to remember the dad from when I was younger. I am very thankful my mom has been as supportive as she can be. I think she always feared if she let my dad go, he would be 100% me and my sister's responsibility. We would never give up on our parents, they never gave up on us and I was pretty obnoxious.

Chapter 11

Brighter Days

My dad would attend church every Sunday, he enjoyed it. I think it honestly helped him through the week. Eventually he was taking lower doses of his medicine. He was actually acting a little like his old self but never 100%. I would take it because it was way better than him lying in bed all day. And he actually would communicate, which is something I have missed, having a decent conversation with my dad.

He felt and looked so much better on less medicine. He helped around the house and cooked dinner again. I was relieved he felt better. My mom still wanted him to stay away from the laundry though. I thought it was funny he would wash everything together.

He was doing things I hardly ever saw before.

The future was looking brighter, he even bought a 4-wheeler. He didn't drive, my mom had gotten full guardianship over him. And when he had a vehicle he would always run into people and get back on the streets. So he didn't ask to have a vehicle too much. He would ride the 4-wheeler back and forth from my mom's house to his brother's and my sister's. We all lived close, so we didn't worry too much about giving him some freedom. That summer of 2010 I would have my third child, a girl. I would continue to stay with him and he would help me with the baby as I did my college assignments. He seemed to be doing great.

He enjoyed helping with the baby. I think he felt a little bit in control. And he would never argue with me to take his medicine. Things were looking better until October, 2010, my husband received a job two hours away. We moved and my cousin took over for a little bit.

Chapter 12

Life Seems Better

They got along well, she would later get another job offer. My mom found a nurse for him that would stay during the day, and he would come stay with me some in Ada. He continued going to the VA and keeping all appointments. He loves interacting with other veterans.

That's why we thought the soldier's home would be perfect for him. But that didn't happen due to the fact that he missed it by one war day, and it was the military that made him the way he was. It was not easy finding nurses to stay with my dad. The VA doesn't pay hardly anything to have one.

My sister, who is a RN, would fill in when the nurse quit and didn't mind at all. She was the boss and he listened. He did have some fits but my sister straightened him out. I was the one that was laid back.

Mainly because even though he couldn't make decisions, I still felt like he could, because he was my dad. You would never think of making decisions for your dad who was in his 50's. At times taking care of him would make me cry out of nowhere. And there have been plenty of times of me asking God why did this happen to our family. He was the dad that would go all out for Christmas, Easter, and Birthdays.

Chapter 13

Bitter Sweet Memories

Never did I think in a million years I would be helping raise my dad. Or that I would be his authority figure along with my sister and mom. I would cry many nights telling God it's not fair, that other daddy's girls still got to have a decent conversation with their dads.

It's not like I could call my dad and tell him anything. He probably would not listen because he was medicated or wouldn't respond. One thing, though, he has always said he loved us and that's what matters. I might not get to have those conversations with my dad but I know he loves me.

The summer of 2013 I would receive the worst call ever. That my dad had been in a 4-wheeler accident and was being air lifted to St Johns. He wasn't in the best of health.

All that medication has side effects, weakening his bones.

My dad flipped the 4-wheeler upon himself and my aunt and uncle who were across the road saw it happen. Thankfully they did see it happen. They called the ambulance and he was on his way to the hospital. But he had broken so many bones and was bleeding internally that he was air lifted to St Johns.

Me and my husband and kids got in the car and headed to Tulsa. It seemed like the longest two hours ever. I was holding back the tears. I was one of the first to arrive and the first to see him. It was horrible, he was in pain from all the broken bones but refused pain medicine, which was the soldier within him.

The doctor on duty was very skeptical of his recovery considering the fact that he was diabetic- type 2. His healing time would be slower and recovery might be impossible. He was placed in the ICU because he was bleeding internally and they couldn't find where he was bleeding.

He ended up on a ventilator which I struggled with seeing him on. It brought me to tears many of times. And my sister, being a nurse, knows the ventilator can be bad due to you can catch pneumonia and die. My dad was still losing blood and on a vent.

They needed to do surgery quick and see why he was losing so much blood. Surgery took place and they successfully repaired his bones and thought that would take care of the bleeding. But it didn't, he received plasma and blood transfusions. By the Grace of God and lots of prayers, and the best physicians and nurses ever, my dad made a full recovery.

Even the doctor did not think he would walk again. But with lots of support and therapy he was walking. Probably way before he should have been. But he still has training of a soldier in his blood to never stay down. It was like the best miracle ever.

His medicine got messed up in the process so he had to be regulated again. He would make his appointments to his doctor in Tulsa to check how he was healing. He made great progress to the doctor's surprise. He would finally lose the wheel chair and cane. Mr. Stubborn at the time would never give up.

Chapter 14

The Recovery and Relief

Never has the term "give up" been in his vocabulary. That's why he was such a great soldier. The year 2014 rolled around and he was told by this one doctor that there was this treatment that they were offering veterans and soldiers with PTSD. They were hyperbaric treatments and it might help with Dad's mental status. We were not familiar with hyperbaric chambers, nor did we totally believe it could help.

Because let's face it, if you suffer with a mental disorder for very long you become what I call brain fogged. So many medicines that control your mental status can have long term effects on the brain. If he was just recently diagnosed with that mental disorder I think it could help drastically. But it was free and who knows, it could have a great outcome. The doctors in OKC donated their time to the veterans, soldiers and many others.

I drove him two hours to take an assessment test. He failed it horribly meaning he might actually benefit from this oxygen treatment. The doctor set him up with a 40-treatment plan three days a week an hour a day. So I would drive him two hours and wait on him.

They first asked me if I wanted to go diving with him. I thought about it and saw the narrow chamber. It reminded me of a submarine you see on TV. I do not like closed in areas, so I never dived with him. The generous doctors dedicated their time to helping people like Dad. The building they operated out of was a donated building. Computers needed to help keep up with progress of treatments. The doctors are retired veterans themselves.

Each treatment I had my doubts that it was even working. He would sleep more without his medicine, which was a good sign, but I still didn't see an improvement with his mind. Sometimes I even struggled to get him to his appointments. He still made his VA appointments and his hyperbaric treatments.

By the 19th treatment I took him to eat afterwards and he made a comment like he used to way back when I was younger. He was eating and dropped his food on his shirt. He said, "Oh crap I'm so messy I missed my mouth." And he was frustrated that he made a mess. I thought my dad was back like 20 years ago.

He always said things like that, I thought nothing of it then. But I was driving and was so happy he said that I almost went off the road. I was laughing so hard he probably thought I was crazy. I would continue to see improvement and he looked better and would continue to say things he used to.

The dad I once knew was showing his old side again. He completed 40 treatments. Even though he wasn't completely back to his old self he was closer than I could ever imagine he would be. Those doctors gave us hope and got him closer to reality than any other doctor who would just medicate the veterans. He still has a nurse who is very good to him, she takes him places and keeps him in line.

Will my dad ever relapse and be on the streets? It's a possibility. I pray it doesn't ever happen again. As a veteran with PTSD you never know what the situation will be. I am hoping that the VA will do more and address the problems of soldiers sooner.

If we Americans are more active in helping our soldiers and veterans we could prevent so much heartache. It's the least we can do since they served for our freedom. We could save soldiers and veterans from snapping and hurting others or themselves. We could help them get the care they need and deserve. They need a chance at a normal life like everyone else gets.

They give us respect when we don't deserve it. You will hardly ever see a veteran asking for help, only for a job. They are trained to work and are willing to work. But they are turned down more than anyone else.

There are more veterans than documented with PTSD. They never seek help or they are unaware of the problem they have. We treat illegal citizens better than our veterans, it sounds crazy but look around and you will see the truth. Some families leave the veterans because of the actions of the veteran. And they become homeless and can't find a job, they feel worthless.

The story has no happy ending or bad ending. My dad still has 24-hour care and still takes his medicine. And Dad and other veterans still get the horrible healthcare from the VA. The VA needs to step up and help more. No veteran should ever be homeless. America should do all it can for everyone that served our country.

www.ingramcontent.com/pod-product-compliance
Lightning Source LLC
Chambersburg PA
CBHW060617030426
42337CB00018B/3094